Boomy
the
Bittern

Pam Earnshaw

Illustrated by Sally Mills

Sally Mills

Pam Earnshaw.

CRANTHORPE
MILLNER
PUBLISHERS

First published by Cranthorpe Millner Publishers (2023)

ISBN 978-1-80378-087-0 (Paperback)

www.cranthorpemillner.com

Cranthorpe Millner Publishers

How this book came about...

Bitterns became extinct in Britain due to hunting and the drainage of their wetland habitat. Indeed, in the Middle Ages, they were widely eaten as a popular Sunday lunch!

So, how were they enticed back?

Bitterns need a particular wetland habitat in order to survive, with pools, lakes and ditches where they can fish, and reedbeds where they can nest and stay camouflaged. In the nineties, a small isolated number of bitterns were discovered to have returned to breed in the wetlands of Eastern England. However, after peat extraction ceased in certain places on the Somerset Levels and Moors, in the west of England, conservation organisations such as the RSPB, Natural England and Somerset Wildlife Trust acquired some of this land, to use the opportunity to create a wetland in Somerset. Between them, they established a huge mosaic of different habitats, creating one of the largest wetlands in Europe, which came to be known as the Avalon Marshes.

Local people were enlisted as volunteers to help create a landscape suitable for bitterns. From 1995 to 2007 Sally was Site Manager at one of the nature reserves, and Pam was one of the regular volunteers who carried out a huge variety of tasks.

It took many years for the bitterns to find the new wetland that was created… but they did, and they are now well established in the Avalon Marshes, along with many other species, both flora and fauna, making the marshes a very special place to visit. If you do, and are lucky enough to hear the booming sound of the bittern, you will never forget it. It thrums through the air like no other call.

The threat once posed to bitterns, with regards to the drainage of wetlands for building and farming for example, is no longer strong. However, this story brings home the ongoing need to protect these special creatures and their habitats, especially given the increased pressure on wildlife worldwide and the effects of climate change. Our story is a 'can do'; a positive example of how humans can help to preserve the incredible world around us and the creatures we share it with.

Want to know more about this amazing bird? The information page at the end will help you do just that.

Boomy the bittern
lived in a wetland.

A wetland of pools,
islands,
ditches and dykes.

There were reeds in the wetland,
where Boomy could hide,
and ditches where he could feed.

He was happy sloshing,
sploshing and plopping around.

1

Boomy loved to hear the
sh... sh... sh... pl... od,
sh... sh... sh... pl... od,
sh... sh... sh... pl... od
as he squelched in the water.

He loved the sound of eels,
frogs and fish,
as they sh... sh... sh... l... ooped
into his mouth.

Sh ... sh... sh... l... oop,
sh... sh... sh... l... oop,
Scoop...

It was easy to scoop
food up with his long beak.

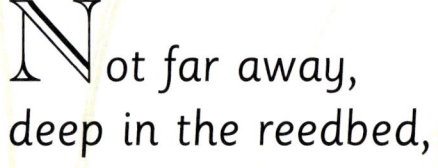

Not far away,
deep in the reedbed,

young bitterns were waiting to be fed,
hiding in the reeds.

They were Boomy's chicks.
They were hungry,
not big enough to find their own food.

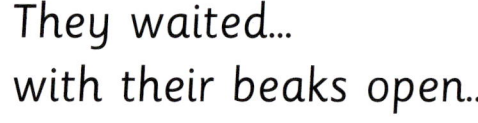

They waited...
with their beaks open...

4

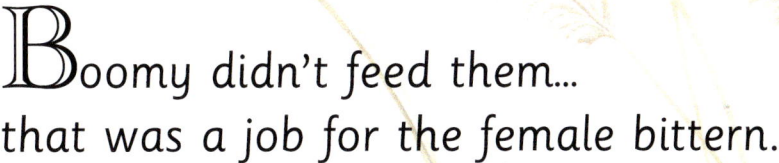

Boomy didn't feed them...
that was a job for the female bittern.

She was close by, also busy,
feeling and fishing in the water,
probing with her long beak.

As she searched
for juicy bits
for her chicks to eat,

she was always on the lookout for danger...

If danger comes,
quick as a flash,
bitterns can flick
into a stick shape.

A shape like a stem
that can hide them
in the reeds.

Today there was no danger,
and the chicks were still being fed.

6

Boomy was on the far side
of the wetland,
ready to go for a fly.

Stretching his wings,
he went high, high into the sky.

He looked like an owl with streaky feathers
and long droopy legs.

Always looking, always listening.

He flew through the air,
over the chicks' nest.

He proudly watched the young bitterns
being looked after by their mother.

But as he flew,
he heard a sound,
a sound he didn't like...

Brm brm... brrmmm.

Brm brm... brrmmm.

Brm brm... brrmmm.

A sound he really didn't like.

As he looked down
Boomy saw big lorries bringing long pipes.

He felt the noises shuddering the air.

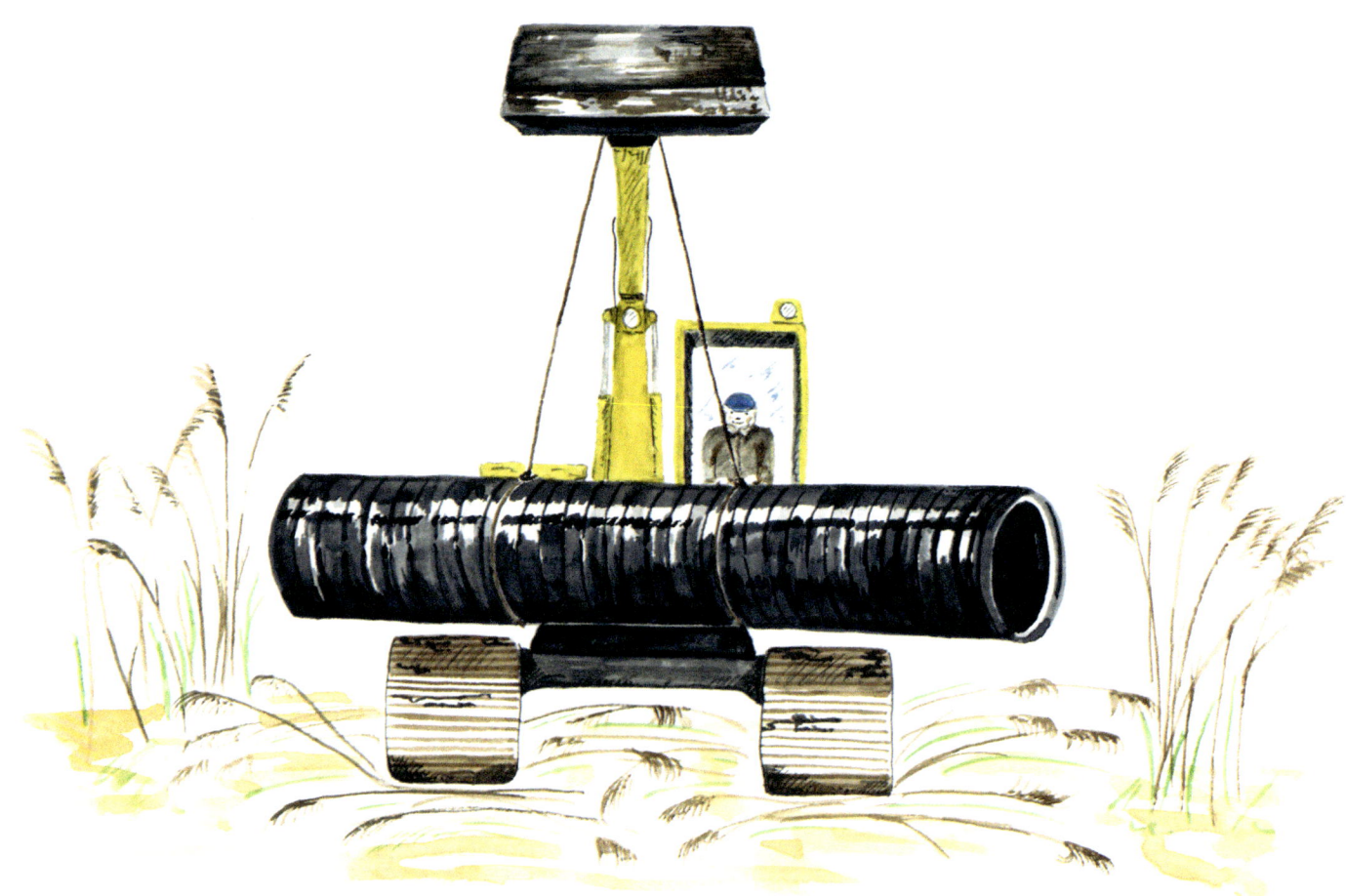

What was going on?

Boomy saw diggers
digging trenches.

He saw cranes
lifting the pipes
and lowering them down
into the trenches.

Boomy had seen things like this before.
He was afraid the wetland would dry up.

He was afraid the pipes would take all the water
out of the reedbeds.

He was afraid the reedbeds would dry up,
afraid there would be
no more frogs and fish,
no more food
for the young bitterns!

No more food for him
and his family!

They needed the wetland...
it was their home!

Boomy flew back
over the young bitterns.

The young bitterns were
not yet big enough to fly...

what could he do?

They could not stay where
there was no water...

He drifted down, landing gently, careful not to land too near to the nest.

Predators were always on the lookout for juicy young bitterns to eat.

Boomy's big powerful bittern claws made it easy
to travel secretly through the stiff, thick, dense reedbed...

to the young bitterns.

He was quite near now.

As he landed, his clever claws snatched the reeds with lightning speed.

Boomy flashed through the reedbed.

Clutch and stride,
clutch and stride,
clutch and stride.

The reeds rustled, bent and cracked,
as if the wind was blowing through them.

Boomy the bittern
was now very close to the nest.

How could he tell them
that danger lay ahead?

He raised himself up,
drew in as much breath as he could...
then...

booooooooooom...
booooooooooom...
boomed with all his might.

Discover how you can
boom like a bittern
on the back page.

17

The chicks still sat
with their beaks wide open,

too young to know about danger.

They sat waiting... waiting...

then gobbling... gobbling.

The female bittern was too busy feeding them
to heed Boomy's call.

Boomy watched.

He knew they had to leave.

He knew they had to go
before the wetland dried out.

But where?

Would there be time for the chicks to grow strong?

Time for the chicks to grow big enough to fly?

Would there be time to find another home
before the reedbeds went dry?

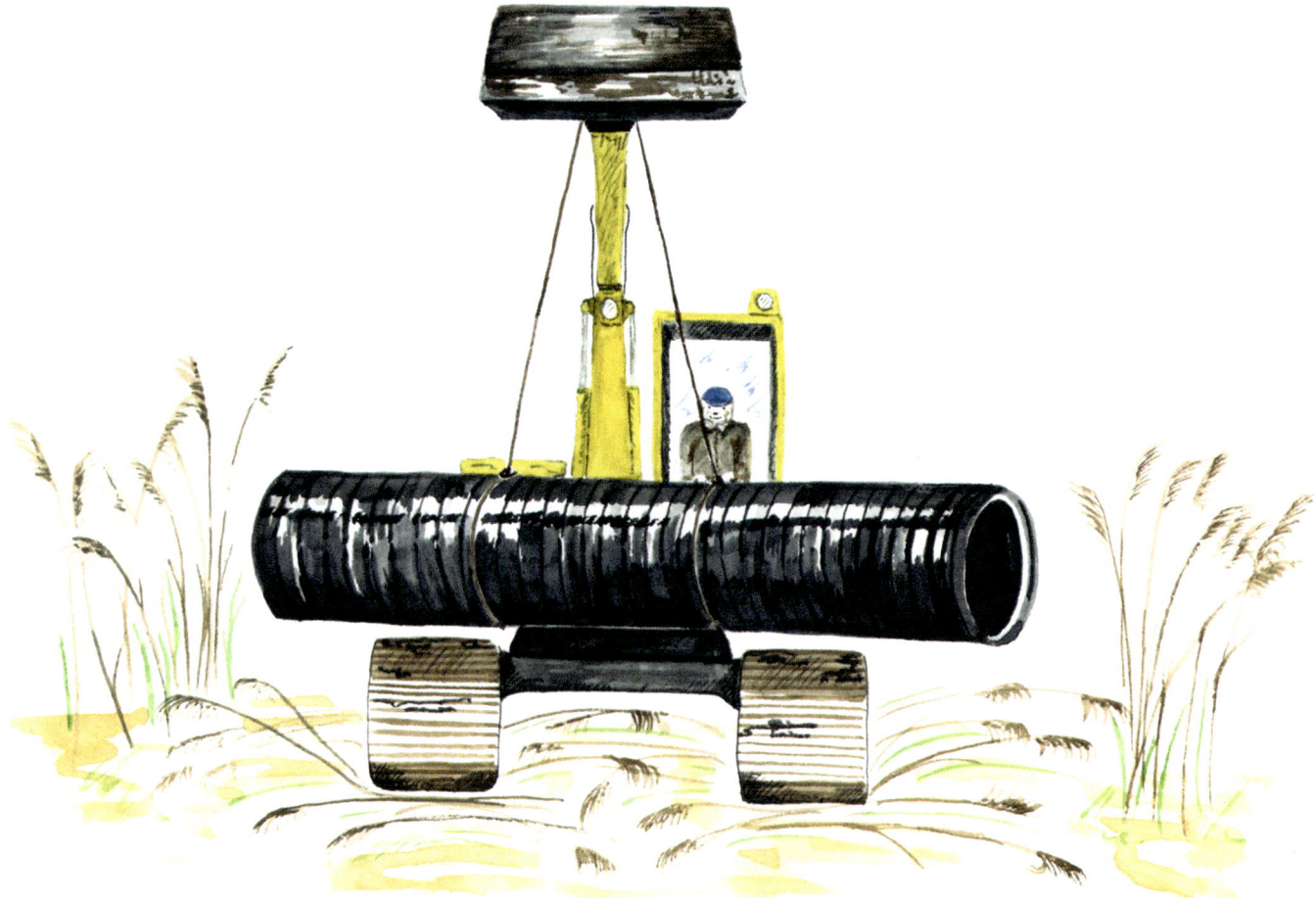

They had to have reeds to hide in and ponds to fish in.

Boomy boomed again.

Boooooooooom... boooooooooom.

This time the female bittern did stop feeding the chicks.

She knew something was wrong.

She gathered them closer.

She listened harder.

She heard Boomy's boom and the strange noises...

Brrmmm.
Brrmmm.

Where could they go to be safe?
Where could they live?

The young bitterns were much too little to fly,

but they had to have reedbeds to hide in

and water to fish in,
or they would die!

The weeks went by, and Boomy was worried.

The wetland was drying out,
and food was harder to find.

But the chicks were a lot bigger,
and they would soon be able to walk and learn to fly.

The female bittern had fed them well.

Brrmmm... brrmmm.

The digger noises were very, very close now.

The bitterns could hear the workers shouting...

But the reeds still kept the young bitterns hidden.

They were growing fast.

They were nearly ready to fly.

Dumph da dumph.
Dumph da dumph.
Dumph da dumph.

That was the water pump.

The bitterns were running out of time.
All the water was being pumped away.

Boomy was watching
the other wildlife
that lived
in the wetland.

Had they sensed the danger?

27

Suddenly,
lots of birds filled the sky.

Swirling,

flapping,

quacking,

calling and cackling.

They rose higher.

Up, and up and away they flew,
away from the drying wetland...

Where were they going?

28

Boomy decided to follow them...

Up, and up and away they flew,

Over the hills, over the town,

over the moors, over the fields.

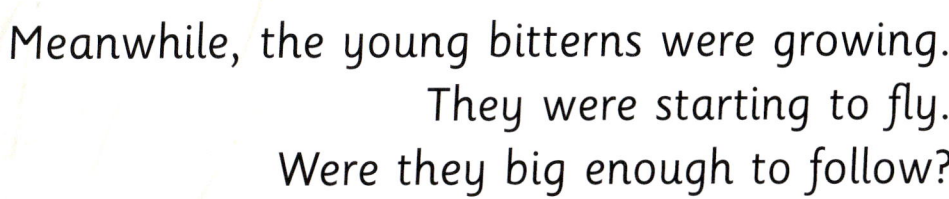

Meanwhile, the young bitterns were growing.

They were starting to fly.

Were they big enough to follow?

Where were they going
Boomy wondered?

Over big green spaces.
Far, but not too far.

They began to circle...
they were getting ready to lan

30

Boomy looked down.

Could it be?

He thought he saw...

was it water?

Yes, it was... **water!**

... but would there be places to hide?

... would there be reedbeds?

Glide and sink, glide and sink.

Boomy floated down,

circled and looked,

circled and looked,

and then, he saw...

Water, lots of water.

Clear water with fish,
frogs and muddy banks.

Rustling reedbeds
and lots of secret places to hide!

NATURE
RESERVE

They had everything they needed.

A perfect new home
for all the bitterns.

33

Boomy had found a perfect new home.

Bittern facts:

Bitterns are well known for the booming sound they make. If you want to know what a bittern sounds like, you can try and make the sound of a bittern at home, by blowing over the top of an empty glass bottle.

The scientific name for bitterns is *Botaurus stellaris*. They are a large, heron-like bird with a long-pointed bill and distinctive golden-brown mottled plumage. Bitterns are shy and secretive, with plumage that blends well into their reedy home.

Most adult bitterns range in size from 70-80cm.

Bitterns are still very rare, and their main UK breeding strongholds are in East Anglia, Lancashire and the Somerset Levels. They live in wetlands and marshes with extensive reedbeds.

Bitterns can be found in 27 European countries, with 89% of them living in just 10 of these countries. The European breeding population is estimated at 10,000-11,700 pairs, with a further 10,000-30,000 pairs in Russia and 30-500 pairs in Turkey.

There were nearly 200 breeding bitterns in the UK on the 2021 red list: www.birdlife.org/news/2021/10/14/press-release-european-red-list-of-birds-2021/

Old quirky names for bitterns include: 'barrel-maker', 'bog-bull', 'bog hen', 'bog-trotter', 'bog-bumper', 'mire drum', 'butter bump', 'bitter bum', 'bog blutter', 'bog drum', 'boom bird', 'bottle-bump', 'bull of the bog', 'bull of the mire', 'bumpy cors', and 'heather blutter'. Maybe you could make up some new ones?

What do bitterns need*?

1. Large wetlands.
2. A wet reedbed, (20–30% of the site must be open-water pools, meres or a network of open ditches, with the right conditions to support a sustainable fish population in summer and winter, with fish such as rudd and eel which will use wet reedbed margins).
3. The water level across the reedbed should be at least 20 cm deep and should not fluctuate dramatically.
4. Areas of reedbed free from disturbance to allow nesting, which also remain wet for a sufficient period to allow chicks to be fed and fledge.
5. Some profiled open-water reedbed edges should always stay wet to allow access to food.
6. Refuge areas from predators, a wet reedbed is more likely to deter most native UK mammalian predators than a dry reedbed.

*As identified in the paper 'Bitterns and Bittern Conservation in the UK' by Andy Brown, Gillian Gilbert and Simon Wotton, British Birds 105, February 2012, 58–87. Accessible at: www.researchgate.net/publication/283080549_Bitterns_and_Bittern_Conservation_in_the_UK

See also:
www.rspb.org.uk/birds-and-wildlife/wildlife-guides/bird-a-z/bittern/
www.wildlifetrusts.org/wildlife-explorer/birds/herons-egrets-and-spoonbill/bittern
https://app.bto.org/birdfacts/results/bob950.htm

BV - #0048 - 280323 - C39 - 210/210/3 - PB - 9781803780870 - Gloss Lamination